JUST BREATHE

LATONYA S. HICKS

authorHOUSE®

AuthorHouse™
1663 Liberty Drive
Bloomington, IN 47403
www.authorhouse.com
Phone: 1 (800) 839-8640

Published by AuthorHouse 08/22/2017

ISBN: 978-1-5462-0526-5 (sc)
ISBN: 978-1-5462-0525-8 (e)

Library of Congress Control Number: 2017912900

Print information available on the last page.

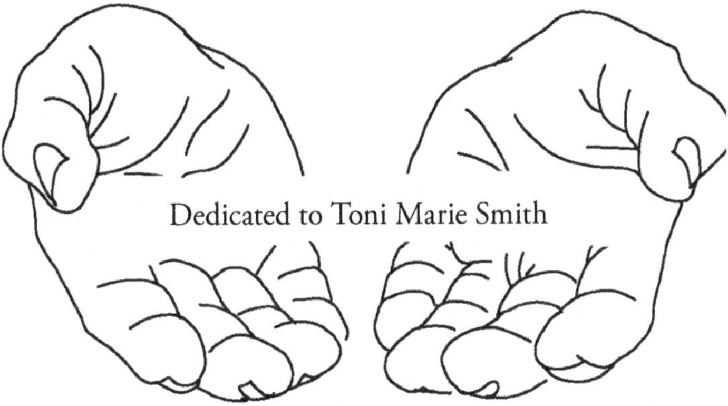

Dedicated to Toni Marie Smith

author's desktop

I found my voice. Not the one that existed when I was trying to please everyone, but the one that surfaced after I realized who I am. For so long, I would wait for confirmation from others to move forward. I was afraid of being judged. I was afraid to stand in my own light. I allowed people to control my light switch. I let them turn it on and off when they chose. I hid behind their words and their opinions. I felt that I needed acceptance in order to succeed, but I was wrong. The hardest challenges came when I was alone. No one was there. At first, it frightened me. I felt lost. It was then that I realized that I had power to move and exist in my own light. I was strong enough to stand alone. It was then that I discovered who I really am.

Now, I am living for me. I am walking in my purpose, no longer looking over my shoulder or tilting my head to catch the hearsay. I write my truth and I speak what's in my heart. I can't worry about the things that I can't control. There will always be negativity, but I have learned to drown it out. I have to live my truth.

This is a journey of self-discovery, an art of reinvention. The beginning of the journey is self-love. True self-love shapes our inner image and then resonates on the outside. I will no longer be afraid to be myself, empower myself and encourage myself.

Your life is your own. Love it deeply. Live it boldly. And in doing so, someone else will be inspired to do the same. I love you.

let it come
it's meant to come
and if it leaves
let it leave
just let it flow
and fill the air
it is yours
that's why it's there

-this moment

contents

know your gift
use your gift
share your gift
own it

glory

i laid many days in that hospital bed
some of those days i wished i was dead
pain in my body and aches in my head
still can't believe i survived that hospital bed

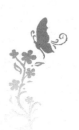

faith

she was like roses
set in harms way
neglected of water
on the warmest days
and yet she still blossomed
and never vanished
her shield was too strong
to ever be damaged

cover

some people think that outside image
is where true beauty starts
but a lot of people have colorful shells
with an ice cold black heart

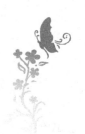

timing

someday
you'll mean the world
to someone

wait
be patient
never settle

certitude

don't look at my yesterday
i was behind closed doors
fumbling with words
not knowing what i stood for

don't judge me by yesterday
those are old scars
i was convicted by my wounds
i was locked behind bars

but judge me by today
i am free
today

ice

if love is what
we give so freely
why is it hard
shouldn't it be easy

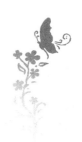

monarch

real queens inspire
they don't put each other down
instead they admire
the diamonds on one another's crowns

the gift

dear mother
even though they talked about you
tore you down and cursed you
for their name's sake
i will continue to prove why
having me wasn't a mistake

soar

we were all created to do
more than we have ever imagined we could
so always dance
and take a chance
and if believe you can fly
leap

repeat

i am beautiful
in my own skin
i know it now
i knew it then
i love myself
and that's why i win
i am beautiful
i'll say it again

solely

i thought i needed a man
to kill the spider above my shelf
but being alone has taught me that
i can kill it all by myself

pearls

don't search her outer beauty
she shines from within
she's poised with grace and elegance
it's the magic inside of her skin
and when she stands to walk
people become unsure
she's composed of the finest minerals
and she's electrifyingly pure

esteemed

he thinks that telling me i'm beautiful
will draw him nearer
but i already know what i look like
i have a mirror

zeal

love is not a
man or a woman
love can't be placed on a shelf
love is not materialistic
love is God
and self

covenant

promise me this

you won't lose yourself
chasing what if's

dimples

he said he loved me
and so i stayed
but that kind of love
almost put me in the grave

the mantle

remember when you cried at night
and no one saw your tears
remember when you shook inside
and no one felt your fears
and remember when you came out of it
refreshed and mentally strong
it's because you had HIS covering
God was right there all along

pedal

and the key to surviving is
learning to balance the
good and the bad, the
happy and the sad
realizing that life has no loyalty
to either one

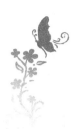

acceptance

the scars that have been
assigned to me
will no longer be
defined by me

the reward

far too often we voice our pain
to prove a point for personal gain
we forfeit peace and become violent
not realizing the victory was in remaining silent

anew

i am not
who i was before
just ask yesterday
it doesn't know me anymore

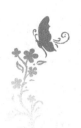

careful

when you love yourself
you love your curves and
all of your waves

you're confident enough to
be yourself
you break rules and misbehave

evolution

growth comes by
having the courage to get up
you have to be the soaring eagle
not the sitting duck

raise

don't let a bad day question your being
you were made to stretch
and expand
and expound
you will always land
with your feet on the ground

tides

i can't accept mediocre anymore
either we're going to crash
or set waves to the shore

aura

i think my presence does something
in ways that others can't compare
every time i walk into a room
people always stare

him

he has the power to exhilarate her
she desires him insomuch
he's secured a place inside of her
that no other man can touch

false hope

an inch of hope
only seen through a microscope
will keep us anticipating love
forever

walls

don't look as if you're shocked
or try to act surprised
you took the sacred needle
and pierced it through my thighs

you sat and watched me build them
you uttered not a sound
and now that they've been cemented
don't you dare try to tear them down

habits

when pain is too familiar
happiness is always distant
we try to save what we think we have
all the while it was nonexistent

sparkle

don't forget to love yourself
be sure to put you before anyone else
open your hand and let if fizzle
bring it with you and then leave a little

generational curse

maybe that's why it hurts
it could be the ultimate sacrifice of
debts unpaid before you

maybe you're just the recipient of
your ancestors' fall
maybe it's not your fault
at all

bankrupt

money can buy things
that love can't offer
and love can give things
that money could never afford

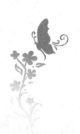

wait

if he doesn't have time to
explore your soul
don't let him consume
what makes you whole

you are a woman
of contemplation
don't compromise your expectation

recommence

i don't care that you have
a heart of gold
do me one better
show me your soul

sharing

don't hold your thoughts
they were created by design
just hold your words
you'll know when it's time

celibate

you'd think that it was folded
or sewn in a way that not even
urine could trickle down my leg

it seems as if it was stitched
or sealed with guerilla glue
because no one has visited there
since you

stare

i never ever blinked my eyes
i just watched very closely
had a habit of always picking men
who never ever chose me

know your truth
own your truth
tell your truth
speak it

hopeful

we look for things we cannot have
in places where they'll never exist
we wipe away tears that are never seen
to hide our loneliness

we reach for stars that seem too high
in search of our true light
we don't let worry spoil our dreams
we've vowed to never lose sight

armor

when you feel like you're a failure
it's all inside of your head
lift up to fight off the demons
then go on back to bed

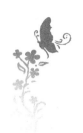

irony

isn't it funny that
when you're alone at night
you cry over the very things that you
urge others to be
strong about

impact

they run around in circles
flipping over chairs
they check their clocks and watches
wishing you'd be there
they pace the floor assured that
you'll come because you care
you must understand your impact
it is your pain that they bear

purpose

don't be upset at doors confined
finding the key may take some time

don't be disgruntled by what you see
not every eye can consume what will be

don't become upset if he doesn't love you now
maybe he just doesn't know how

just be grateful that you made it through
you were created because the world needed you

pull

stop trying to make him love you
it's ripping you apart
he'll never see the good in you
stop breaking your own heart

flat- footed

it seems these girls are hotheaded
they're too young to have nothing to lose
unbothered by his mental incompetence
yet fascinated by his shoes

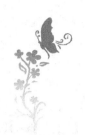

butterflies

i tell myself that i'm over it
my mind is finally convinced
but then he walks into the room
and my body begins to flinch

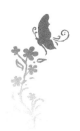

trials

never say what you cannot handle
you don't know what will balance you
because right when you think you've figured it out
life will challenge you

jilted

but weren't you the one who said that
love could not consume us
you bored me with your story of how
we'd never evolve into anything real

and weren't you the one who
left me standing in a puddle of tears
while you walked away
closing the door sternly behind you

i just remember you telling me how you wish you
never met me
so in order for me to move on from here
you have to let me

bearing

it's bold
to pour out your entire soul
to a heart that will never
beat for you

words

it's not what you say
it's how you deliver it
always pack light
and be considerate

science

he couldn't find a
single ounce of love
to give me

how could two hearts
be worlds apart

insufficient

i understand that your road to love
was tough
but i made you my everything
and that wasn't enough

daily struggle

i toss and turn about my gifts
i fight and toil for righteousness
the world is cold and life is hard
and so i tighten my stabled guard

judge me not for i am proud
to stand my ground and speak it loud
i will not change my humbled stance
i've placed my worries in God's great hands

reception

there's energy behind your actions
and life inside of your words
there's vapor in your nostrils
and pain for what is unheard

so when you find your voice
speak and then believe
you have the power to change the world
give and then you will receive

weakness

she had a plan to leave him
she packed her bags while he slept
but at the door, she fell to the floor
covered her mouth and wept

seduction

don't give me those mellow eyes
when i come and sit next to you
we both have tongues
and private thoughts
i know what you're trying to do

staged

they played in a pool of jealousy
for a relationship that the world designed
they never acquired a fire for love
just wasted each other's time

the moving

sometimes the hardest part is
moving forward

the past is familiar
the future is something new
sometimes it's just hard to
move on from what you're use to

acquired taste

he said he liked honeycombs
melanin
and grape leaves
he had an addiction to tropical fruit
yet he was afraid to taste me

belated

where are all of the sweet boys
who open doors
and wonder what real women are looking for

where are the boys
who dare not say too quickly how they feel
because they too, want what's real

where are all the boys who
respect her choice to wait
my mother should have had me sooner
i think i arrived too late

medium

you say you can't
because your mama didn't
you say you're not
because your daddy isn't
but they are like cars
with a front and a rear
they're just the vehicles
that got you here

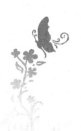

void

just make sure that when you
walk out of that door
you never think about
returning anymore

home

he is long gone from my presence
but my heart often reminds me
that he still has residency
inside of me

extraction

it's funny how you chose to leave
and i have to deal with it
was i that much of a disgrace that you
couldn't even sign the birth certificate

emotional eater

a slice of pumpkin pie would be nice
filled with nutmeg and cinnamon spice
add some marshmallows and chocolate fondue
give me a slice that's big enough for two
i also want milk, can you put in on the rocks
and while you're up, pass me the tissue box

control

he clears his throat
when i talk to men
he rolls his eyes
his ears, he bend

he questions their intent
with hopes of assurance
then pulls me back in
with lack of endurance

silly old me
i should move on but i don't
thinking he'll come around
but he won't

settling

breaking her was his decision
but staying was up to her

domestic

if you keep taking him back
after he batters you
sooner or later
he's going to shatter you

risen

i took a couple of days to
rearrange my thoughts
i played soft music in dark rooms
i packed away memories
and put away reminders

i finally formed a routine
centered in happiness
and peace

i started to feel whole again
distant tears became worthless
then on day twenty-two
he resurfaced

broken

it's okay if she's angry
and if she screams and cries
hell,
you should be happy
that you're still alive

circumvention

he's not my type
never has been and
never will be

he walks past me everyday
trying to get me
to look his way

i feel so bad
i'm forced to speak
he starts to tremble
his knees get weak

he stares for a while
as we talk on a whim
and when i go home
i think of him

planted

you are beautiful
hear me clear
you can make it
have no fear
look how far you've come so strong
you've been enough all along
God is your strength
he designed you
don't ever let a man define you

seeds

when they are boys:

teach your sons how
to aim for the toilet
not the wall
or the floor

when they become men:

teach your sons
to aim for whatever direction
is pivotal

but most importantly
teach them that
condoms aren't invisible

adultery

not all widows
are sad widows
if their spouse's fate
was of sheets
and pillows

expunged

why can’t i erase
this moment this day
why can’t it all just go away
i’ve got ears
i heard them say,
“he don’t want her, anyway”

seasons

it's never this dry out
sometimes the sand washes to shore
and mother nature allows the rain to
touch my tongue
but the winds aren't strong

and the breeze is free
like palm trees and dandelions
the sky disconnects from the clouds
but it has never been this loud

too odious for an umbrella
its luminosity has embedded pearls
of sunshine in the form of sweat drops
but it's never been this hot

i can breathe nature
i can taste elephant ears
and funnel cakes

it looks like rain dipped in gold
it appears to be an imprint of a rainbow's glow
it feels like confidence of a lesser bold
but it has never, ever been this cold

picky

i will try anything once
although i'm picky and sometimes blunt
my palate is strict and pleased by few
so just because i'll bite doesn't mean i'll chew
please be careful with what you put in my mouth
i am open to taste, but i won't hesitate to spit it out

trust issues

i don't let strangers come into my home
outsiders throw rocks and neighbors throw stones
i sit on the porch and watch them pass
they look at me once then stare through the glass
no one gets through my front door
no feet except mine will walk on my floor
momma told me when her health was strong
to keep the flies outside where they belong
and so i'm sure to check all of the locks
and ignore them no matter how hard they knock
they want to come in and sit on my chair
use my toilet and suck up my air
but i refuse to let them in
i don't want their company, i don't need a friend
they can hide their rock and drop their stone
i don't let strangers come into my home

done

you've apologized for the lies
and all that you've done to deceive
but i no longer accept your standards for love
just pack your bags and leave

levels

it may sting a little
but it won't cut you
your cloth is like leather
they can't touch you

college graduation

mother, since you weren't there
don't look for accolades
you weren't there to help me cross the street
you won't watch me walk across the stage

manifested pants

and yes i write my dreams
and hold them by the seams
because all it takes is ambition
to bring it all into fruition

blink

usually i'm shy
and wouldn't say hi
but tip the waiter
then meet me in the elevator

soot

beware of the gentle man
who has been burned by his ex
all he wants is frivolous conversations
and meaningless sex

choices

if i stopped striving today
where would that leave me
how could i survive
if i mentally stopped breathing

my dreams would falter
and my goals would die
i wouldn't make a difference
my whole life would be a lie

tonight

tonight, i'll rest in my own thoughts
i won't consume any torn feelings
i wont ponder over broken pavements

tonight i won't blame myself for the mistakes
and the unwanted hurt

tonight
my meditation will be focused on
the building, the climbing
the fulfilling my fantasy

for once, i'll lay all sadness to rest
tonight my focus is me

tomboy

sometimes i want to lose my mind
and express my inner crazy
but then a soft voice tells me to
calm down and act like a lady

student loans

she says that i am nothing
but she's always staring at me
she often calls me stupid
but i'm the one with the degree

we both attended college
in a small town in carolina
but i guess while i was attending class
men were studying her vagina

momma's boy

he wasn't ready to let go and
he showed it
eyes enraged, fists balled

he stood as close as he could
dreading the release that would
change him forever

every minute felt like a second
and every second less than that

he would spend the next few minutes trying to
overindulge in what would be his
last time in bliss

"okay, she said,
it's time for you to see what life is all about"
he cried and wept as she proceeded
to take her left breast out of his mouth

vow

don’t leave me like this
don’t walk away
you said you would stay
so stay

shield

and when you think no one cares
God is always listening

keep talking
you'll get through it

you will always
get through it

continue

i don't know what
i'm doing wrong
i can't tell when i'm
doing it right

all i know is that
the feeling is strong
and so i must continue
to fight

know your worth
show your worth
honor your worth
respect it

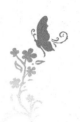

value

i pity the fool who
hurts me
leaves me
rejects me and
doesn't understand my worth
you are an enigma
how could you allow something
so precious
to get away

insomnia

at night my pillow takes beatings
and my sheets get all wrapped up
in my feelings

surface

don't ponder your thoughts
focus on the lesson
they'll never accept you
once they feel threatened

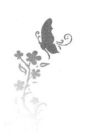

moving

sometimes life
is just a breath
filled with grit
and loneliness

covered in guilt
by things we've said
we're always replaying
what's in our head

we can't give sadness
too much praise
because after the rain
there are better days

so if you look back
just glance, don't stare
the best is coming
you just gotta get there

dismissed

unrequited love is sad
you miss someone
you've never had

battles

i've ovecome things
i never thought i could
i fought certain battles
i never thought i would
one thing about life is that
it's never really steady
so you're never prepared
you're never really ready

lifeline

i need to come down
i need to come down
somebody please save me

i can't stop my lips from bending
they both keep extending

all he does is say my name
and i just melt it's such a shame

somebody save me from myself
i can't seem to think of anything else
it's his smile and beautiful eyes
his masculine hands and muscular thighs

i need to come down
i need to come down
i wish that he would save me

know your strength
show your strength
embrace your strength
own it

clouds

you're waiting for the pain
to go away
it seems to get worse
every day

the pain is a storm
a form of bad weather
keep looking up
it will get better

power

she is fierce
and kind
she leaves no wheels unturned
she is fire
burning of ambition
and creativity
she embraces her femininity
and walks with her head high
she is amazing
structured from the strongest root
embedded in the toughest grain
because she knows that she is
confident and
resilient
her ears are inclined to
take it all in
she is love
she is strength
and she will never settle

achilles heel

he angered her all of the time
missed phone calls
unanswered texts
it hurt her heart
and caused tears to
flow like a river
with sad tides
of continuous motion
and then when she was tired
and could no longer manage
he'd know just what to say to
un-do all of the damage

hush

if i can't trust you with my lie
or let you hold my truth
what good would
telling you my secret do

love

it empowers
it hurts
it angers
it penetrates
it threatens
it crushes
it stings
it soothes
it pushes
it urges
it tastes
it invades
it lasts
in its rarity
love

charles

he is like a sweet rose
lost inside of a dozen
i'd pick the one that favors him
and trash the ones that doesn't
i've never known a love so sweet
he has so much of my heart
i remember touching him while she was pregnant
i've loved him from the start

caution

be careful
once you speak those words
my ears will fold
my heart will freeze
and you will be nothing
but a monster
to me

incomprehensible

it's not that i'm weak
it's not that i'm strong
it's just that nothing
can break me
and you will never
understand that

first

today is your day
not his or hers
push all negativity out
and focus on the good that you have
the joy that you deserve
and the life that you're chasing after
today is your day
you're the only one that matters

burned

he said to write
and leave your mark
i reached for the pen
the room was dark
but day had come
and midnight was gone
i had no idea that
that the lights were on

reception

if she loves you
let her
don't question her sentiment
or try to shadow her judgment

if she desires you
let her
don't push her away
because you're concerned about tomorrow
or what others may say

admire the twinkle that you've placed in her eye
allow her smile to
arouse you
because it's you
she sees something
amazing
in you

keepsake

he is like a breath of fresh air
in the cruelest weather
i want to poke a hole in my soul
and let him sip forever

slipped

i felt i'd always been so focused
when i started slipping, people noticed
i had to keep a smile in the wind
with no room for doubt or to start again
as though i made my own bed soft
as if my courage was kept aloft
but sometimes we all become weak
we hit a block, an unreached peak
it happened to me on a rainy day
away from home, ten miles away
i pedaled sternly to faced the challenge
but along the journey, i lost my balance

masking

always remember that no one is perfect
not one being is ever so true
you don't have to try to be perfect
just focus on being the real you

maturity

time doesn't afford you privilege
and words don't make you clever
grey hair is not what defines you
age doesn't make it any better

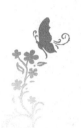

roots

the world sees you smiling
it helps you hide your truth
but when you plant your seed in the soil
make sure that your tree bears fruit

content

i am
awakened to newer heights
asleep to past behaviors
and desires
no longer do i yearn for
that which does not accept me
or for that which
rejects me

i am naked
completely bold
and de-robed
i bear everything
from my clothes
to my soul

i am nothing
but a voice and a
sound
slightly abased
more so
abound

milk

because we are the ultimate source
and we supply it
why do we decide to lend our good
instead of making them buy it

love drug

its fills the air
and makes you smile
it's such
a beautiful
thing

but when you begin
abusing it
you start
to feel
its sting

nostrils

and if she falls
and bumps her head
let her make
her own bed
we're quick to judge
and call her names
shake our heads
and pity her shame
just let her learn
and let it sting
when you were young
no one could tell you a thing

reserved

he cared not to stare at her
as she wiped away her tears
she stood
cold
freezing to the touch
and he turned away from her
afraid that she may grab his inner emotion
that could
ultimately make him stay
he was convinced that he would return again
but not now
later
life seemed harder yet
easier without her

love felt empowering
but from a distance
he wanted not for her feelings to change
but for them to freeze
just like her skin, to the touch
and as he took the first step to
walk away
he also took a deep breath
his legs gained momentum
for he could feel her stare
as he faced the cold air
he thinks she'll wait right there
but he didn't understand how rare
she is

minutes

she says

“he’ll never love you
stop wasting your time”

i say

“but I still love him
it will fade when it is time”

tainted

he says that i'm too picky
but with all of the deception and lying
manipulation and disguises
abuse and distress
diseases and skeletons
upsets and misfits
promiscuity and dander
misogynistic thoughts
perversion and confusion
pain and past hurts
i think i'm doing just fine

stand

your lap is my new favorite place
your lips are my best sharing space
and when you leave i bend my lips
i pull out no chairs
i'd rather not sit

mesmerized

i don't want the kind of love
that keeps him calling at ten past midnight
i want the kind that glistens his eyes
the kind that keeps him staring in my path
even long after i've exited the room

solitary

how could it be that
i've managed to
trample
trip and
fall
but he feels
absolutely
nothing
at all

completion

it's the cycle of life
that presses repeat
it's like a pulse
that skips a beat
divide it by ten
then reduce to half
proceed to add two
and then do the math
the answer confirms
the press and repeat
that makes the equation of life
complete

waste

dear love
present love
past love
love that
i thought was love
but never was
i wish that a single index finger
down my throat could
force you out of me
so that i could simply
and easily
flush you away
forever

disparity

we often criticize love
as if it's some kind of
poison
but love is never complicated
the falling apart is

master

i doesn't matter what they've told you
you've jumped over bridges
you've put out fires
your life hasn't been easy
but look at you
pushing forward
moving forward
and putting it all behind you
wipe those tears
you've conquered your worst fears

create your life
live your life
cherish your life
share it

girl

my body might not be the best
i know i'm different from the rest
i always pause before i go
and yet somehow i steal the show
clever men stare and beat their drum
wondering where i come from
women bicker about my presence
they don't understand my planted essence
my smile is average
my tone is soft
my thoughts are high
and so aloft
i may not be the prettiest in the world
but i still wouldn't trade me for the world

dumping ground

i'd like for the sky to always stay blue
i'd like for the wind to make me anew
i'd like a lily to float in my tea
i'd like for joy to take control of me
i don't want sadness or gloomy days
i don't want feelings that aren't a phase
the burden's too heavy, weight's too strong
it's so far from the truth and seems so wrong
i just want simple to the core of every bone
i want all strings to leave me alone

scared

you stopped
paused completely
and embraced fear
you couldn't see the end

the surface
must have startled you
the unknown
must have created shivers
and emulated quivers
that never really existed

the end is promised
don't be deceived
stop being fearful
start to believe

penalty

if you hold back on your future
when you have so much to give
you pass on what you stand for
and forgo your chance to live

the imparting

most of the time it eats at me
until i release it
it awakens me out of my sleep
and causes my heart to drum harder
with passion

in essence
it's my reminder that
i must always remember where i come from

premise

how can you build a promising tomorrow
when negativity is being spoken
how could you speak of joy and peace
when your foundation of love is broken

stray

and when he comes knocking
and ringing your doorbell
remember the constant pain
and how he put you through hell

never let him in
again

the release

you have to abandon what you want
in order to get what is yours
you won't know
until you let go

association

the rain and the clouds will come to you
but so will the sun
so don't just plan for the misery
you have to prepare the fun

italy

what's the point of
dancing with no pants
in rome
if after
you have to get dressed
alone

ruined

why do you want me
is it to paint on
my empty canvas or to
create music from my soft notes
are you interested in
visiting my dwelling place to
stay a while
or pirouette around
my temple
why are you here
are you taken by my
stance to finally stand
what is your motive
why are you here
leave me alone
let me
and my empty canvas
be

sticky

when he's around
i feel so
gooey
my insides become so
sticky and
gluey
as if i'm calm
and slightly
groovy
his presence
it just
does something
to me

play on words

what angered you most
wasn't the jam or the toast
but the butter that was spread
in between

empty couch

thanks for not being here to wipe my tears
and for not showing up when you should have
thanks for allowing me to go through life wondering who
you were
and if you would have loved me
thanks for not even attempting to be a part of my life
for the missed birthdays and holidays
and the empty couch that comforted me when i got my first
heart break
but i think it's safe to say that you were right
in assuming that i wouldn't need you
because i didn't

midnight

keep pushing even if you cry
trust that everything will be alright
it's only for a season and in a matter of time
you'll see that everything is going to be fine
out in the shadows where everything looks dark
push though all the smoke and ignite your spark
when sunshine falls short and midnight seems long
remember that trials come to make you strong

experience

it's not the stars in the sky
or the sun shining upon my face
it's not the cool breeze from the ocean
or the sound of gentle tides hitting the docks
it's not even the sweet tune of bustling wind
or the glimpse of a rainbow after the storm
but it's the journey of traveling through life
it's the experiences that i have encountered
it's the knowledge that i take with me everyday
that is what makes it all worth it

gem

why doesn't he like you
let me answer your question
not all men are just flattered by
the pearl that causes erection

the pill

how can you follow
what your idol says
yet not even consider
what the bible says

matches

you said you'd be different
when you got a little power
you surpassed fifteen minutes
and prolonged the hour
so now that you've managed to burn
all of your bridges
who's gonna remove your stitches

the invitation

can you stay
just today
and then maybe tomorrow
i don't want to be alone
i want your embrace
just for today
i want your
kiss on my forehead
as we share laughs
about our past and how we will
never love again
can you be my light
just for the night
because when darkness turns to day
the sun will come
and as we lay
i'll smile and as you look my way
i'll ask again
can you stay

the hater

you want me to apologize
for what i'm saying
and for the art
that i am bleeding

please spare me of
your horrid objection
no one forced you
to keep reading

guilty

i may be sweet
to the nose
but i'm no rose
i'm planted and settled
when the wind blows
i am easily swayed by the air's essence
with my agility
i may be resilient but i'm no lily
sometimes my scent is bitter
a little less warmer than fire
my taste is orange
a little less acquired

so i stand
pretty to the eye
fatal to the touch
sweet to the minute
sour to the hour
i may seem inviting
but i'm no flower

transition

maybe it's something i said
or the way that i wear my hair
maybe it's the seasonal change
from soft winds to strong gusts
it may even be the sun
that seems to appear less
and more less these days
all i know is that he's different
and that he has no interest
anymore

foster child

"hey little girl,
why are you crying
times have changed since then"

"because, I replied,
this life is my home
i might have to go there again"

untamed

you rattled the cage
why are you amazed
i am woman
who is moved
by you

you wanted this
so why are you afraid

you got me going
and now i want to know
just how deep your roar can go

just how immense your passion is
just how much you can give

don't be startled
i want you engaged
with the same enthusiasm
that rattled this cage

and if i touch you here and there
then slowly remove my underwear

keep the courage
the roar and rage
with the same momentum
that rattled this cage

she is mine

along the sides of mellow grass
i think of her
i pick out daisies that resemble her essence
i run my fingers slowly down my face
wondering if my features are like hers
because she is mine
i study my teeth imagining if my smile mirrors hers
she is a lost image
an unknown memory that
dwells inside of my thoughts
she is a distant love
but she is mine
always has been and
always will be

regardless of the disconnect
heedless to our separation at birth
she is mine
and even though she has not been seen in the flesh
i can feel her
i have touched her in my dreams
and she has embraced me
she has caressed my skin
and kissed my nose
and that was enough for me to know
that she is mine

exude

eyes open
chin up
shoulders straight
stand tall
extend your legs

plant your feet
soften your face
now walk as though
you own the place

old scars

your past is just a reminder of
what you have defeated

focus on the future
and how you deserve to be treated

contrast

i'd say that i want my husband
to be just like my dad
but he was the greatest disappointment
i have ever had

breaking point

you think that
she doesn't see you
but she does
she hears your cries
and she recognizes your frustration
because she's frustrated too

you even think that
she doesn't understand you
but she does
and she knows that you feel empty
without her
because she feels empty too
way more than you

but what you need to understand
is that she has found love where you lacked
and she has found peace outside of your attack

and the last time
was the last time
that she would ever take you back

the crave

i want to kiss this amazing man
my forehead touches his nose
please, please say you'll kiss me back
i'll stand on my tiptoes

decade

he sits by the clock as it ticks
and then tocks
waiting for the short hand to move
he had convinced himself that
he can change time
minutes go by
then hours
days
weeks
and then years
steadily, he studies the clock
now 3,650 days later
he is still incomplete
and far from over her

tension

they hate to see you
walk their way
smile even harder
love on them anyway

cemented

i've been told that i'm as cold as ice
they say it's because of the burning
the mental debris has permanently
scarred me

i've been told that i'm old
in spirit and in truth
they say that pick up lines don't
work on me anymore
like i've been here before

but i'm just guarded
i've crossed my heart and
hoped to love many times but
nothing

i'm empty
not a pinch nor a sting
so if you were looking to become numb by me
don't worry
you won't feel a thing

feelings

i'll never admit it
when they ask me
but i still look your way
when you walk past me

i have too much pride
to tell the truth
but i made a mistake
by passing on you

the shining

i know i'm fierce
i know i'm strong
i've been dim
for far too long

i have the power
i sing the praise
from now on it's sunshine
and brighter days

i know i'm fierce
i know i'm strong
when you hear me singing
just sing along

the storm

he softened the blow for me
he wanted to make sure the words that
escaped his tongue were soft
and gentle
he spoon fed me the nouns of places and things
he created room for the most vibrant adjectives
and there i stood
flummoxed by his ability
to love on me thoroughly
and intensely
but when it was my turn to return the favor
i blurted my feelings with no chaser

the jealousy

you swing your hips
just in time
the men are coming
and they are fine
you sway in motion
looking for a sign
your rhythm is good
but it ain't mine

one glimpse

no matter how hard you looked
how in focused it appeared
you still couldn't manage to
put it into perspective

your squint made things a little more appealing
but only for a minute
blurriness settled in
causing your anger to

convert into frustration and then into animosity
yet and still your eyes deceived you
you pushed a little harder
this time taking a few steps forward

hoping that you would make the image
into full color like it use to be
what existed now were memories of yesterday and
your brain waves trying to convince your mind that

it will happen again
that you will be able to catch a glimpse
of the beauty that you let slip
through your fingertips

but the harsh reality
that lingers and will find its place
is that you will never again be able to
touch her beautiful face

fractured

there are some doors
that i will never reopen
i simply refused to change the locks
after he broke them

time

life is not like money
we don't have the option to borrow
instead life is not promised
we might not even have tomorrow

below

her words were broken
by small promises
she leaned in and held on
to every word as if they were golden
she started to feel her lips part
as the cold air hit her teeth
and then her tongue
and finally the back of her neck
its taste was cold
and bitter
but yet she chose to pucker
and press her face against the odds
she waited for the clouds
she stood disavowed
not allowed to go any further
forced to let go of what was
and prepare for what was to come
with pain and anger and malice and rage
she slowly kissed her pain away
and waited for the release
that would meet her
for she realized that her past was
finally beneath her

tiffany

i'll honor you in my thoughts
right now i'll let you rest
you captivated so many hearts
and you always gave your best

my heart won't let me forget
all the greatness you stood for
your strength helped me press reset
on the things that life is good for

discover your peace
own your peace
give a piece
cherish it

Printed in the United States
By Bookmasters